Self-help for Fear and Anger (abridged)

The Recovery Method

by Robert Courtade

Medical disclaimer: This book is not intended to replace professional medical advice. Readers are advised to consult with and follow the advice of health professionals. The ideas presented here were created in the most part by psychiatrist Abraham A. Low, M.D. Some newer *Exposure* therapies for OCD may be at odds with one page of this book.

INTRODUCTION

For years I had problems controlling anger and insecurity. Then a physician referred me to Recovery International. After learning a method, I was usually able to guide myself. It required a lot of effort.

According to the 1995 book *Emotional Intelligence,* by Daniel Goleman, we can develop emotional intelligence with training and education. That book advocated training young people so they would grow into more competent adults using impulse control, persistence and empathy. For decades Recovery International meetings have used a cognitive-behavioral therapy, the "Recovery Method[1]," that produces emotional intelligence.

This book is an attempt to explain self-leadership of fear and anger based on the Recovery Method. The ideas included on the following pages come from the oral tradition of Recovery International meetings, which in turn derive the techniques from the writings, and speeches of psychiatrist Abraham A. Low. In addition, I have included a brief account of other ideas.

While most accounts of therapy do not mention it, Recovery was the second self-help system of cognitive-behavioral therapy after A.A. The therapy meetings founded in the 1930's spread across the USA and overseas. Today, there are over 600 such groups. The techniques work as anger management for those with explosive tempers and offer security for those with anxiety and depression. The methods help those with significant psychological conditions but also help others with minor concerns.

The methods became popular with thousands of people who wished to work on their mental health. Patients found that the system helped. Unfortunately, many people today aren't aware of the program.

An advantage of this self-help therapy is that there is essentially no cost associated with it. An individual can work on his or her mental health without spending a large sum of money. People may train in the system on their own. The local groups are run by non-professionals who are trained in the method. If there is a conflict between the Method and a health professional, the person should defer to the professional.

I am not a physician or a psychologist. My experience with these techniques comes from years of managing anxiety and anger. I am deeply grateful to Recovery International members and the late Abraham A. Low, M.D. for developing the following ideas.

My hope is that this book can explain these therapies simply and clearly for those wishing to improve emotional wellbeing. The techniques provide greater tranquility and peace to those who work at the program. The names mentioned in the book are not those of actual people, but represent the efforts of those who have used the method to make their mental health a business.

CONTENTS

PART 1.   RECOVERY METHOD BASICS

"I hear and forget. I see and remember. I *do* and understand." Confucius

THE BASIC THEORY

At its core, the Recovery Method defines healthy thinking and healthy behavior. In every situation, we have a choice between healthy and unhealthy thoughts and actions.   We achieve emotional self-leadership by discovering and adopting healthy thoughts and behaviors. These contrast the harmful behavior people often instinctively use. The Recovery Method provides a road map for making beneficial choices.

Using this simple premise, a person can begin to work on mental health immediately. It is partly a matter of learning what therapeutic idea pertains to a situation. The entire system can be learned in a couple of weeks. The method does not focus on the theoretical origin of an illness and is a non-Freudian approach. The Recovery Method is not a 12-step program but can complement such programs.

People attending the self-help meetings learn the Recovery Method in several ways. The easiest way to learn is by listening to group examples given by veterans of the method. A member may give an example of an event that caused anger or fear. Next, the person will describe the symptoms the event produced. The member will, then, identify the pertinent thoughts or behaviors that benefit the situation.

For example, a clerk is unpleasant towards Michelle. As a result, Michelle becomes angry, unsettled and tense. Michelle chooses to avoid accusing the clerk and keeps her in perspective. She sees that there is no danger in the situation. Using the method, Michelle adopts thinking that defuses her temper. Before she learned the method, Michelle might have fixated on the clerk's attitude. She avoids an argument not out of kindness to the other person, but instead to help herself.

Another way to learn Dr. Low's method is by reading his books. *Mental Health through Will Training* is his most widely read book. A chapter is often read each week at group meetings.

The sayings or slogans recited at meetings are called the Recovery "**tools**[2]," which together form a system of cognitive and behavioral therapy. Each participant must select, from a number of possible choices, the appropriate technique that will help a situation. The sayings mentioned on the following pages come from the oral tradition of Recovery International. This book includes the most common form but the slogans used vary slightly at different meetings. The tools used orally at Recovery meetings in turn paraphrase the writings and speeches of Abraham Low.

It is a sad fact that many of us don't easily recognize healthy choices and our natural inclination may be to make the choice that generates anger or fear. This is often automatic. We may focus on **right versus wrong**[3] issues that excite. Emotional self-leadership can be so alien that it takes years of practice before it becomes second nature.

Unhealthy thinking includes selfishness, perfectionism, vanity, improbable insecurity, tunnel vision and indecision. Bad behavior includes aggression and lack of resolve.

What is healthy thinking? The goal is to be determined, group-minded, patient and realistic; to keep things in perspective. Good behavior involves treating others with civility, controlling expressions of anger and acting in spite of discomfort. With successful self-leadership, symptoms become less severe. The result is an ability to function at a higher level.

Abraham Low believed that most inappropriate emotions are tempers that he divided into two groups. "**Angry temper**"[4] is temper directed at others. "**Fearful temper**"[5] he defined as temper directed toward the self, including anxiety and self-doubt. An important idea to note is that the two tempers reinforce each other. Angry temper creates tenseness and later fearful temper or regret. Fearful temper can create tenseness as well as defensiveness that can later lead to anger. When analyzing emotional situations, we want to determine which type of temper applies.

The majority of examples of the Recovery Method involve trivialities[6].
We may not always see it, but a lot of upsetting situations are routine. By gaining mastery over trivialities, we gain control over the bulk of our daily lives. We limit symptoms and boost functionality. By gaining daily mastery over symptoms, our relationships and health improve. The greater the effort and adherence to the system, the greater are the chances of personal improvement.

New people sometimes expect focus on remarkable situations. However, the accumulation of many small and medium victories generates dramatic improvement in health. Later, the therapy can be applied to bigger events.

"When one will not, two cannot quarrel."   Spanish proverb

"There are two sides to every question: my side and the wrong side." Oscar Levant

"SYMBOLIC VICTORY"[7]

DAN'S COMMENT: I got home from work. Jane, my wife, asked me to mow the lawn. I told her it could wait till tomorrow, Saturday. I insisted I was right. Jane insisted I was wrong. We argued with a lot of temper. Our feelings were strong and we were tense with each other for several days.

***

   Dan and Jane had a disagreement over a triviality. Each person felt a need to prevail in the argument, which is what Recovery refers to as the quest for symbolic victory. What was lost was perspective since the argument was about a triviality. The couple also lost their group focus. Both reverted to being selfish. Humility was replaced by vanity.
   The salient point is that mental health is always most important and winning an argument is not usually so important. Right versus wrong issues are often absurdities, especially compared to health.

"The wisdom of the wise, and the experience of ages, may be preserved by quotation." Isaac D'israeli, English author.

"SPOTTING"

Dr. Low described "**spotting**"[8] as the process of analyzing an emotional situation to determine which ideas or tools might help. A mechanic picks the correct tool from a toolbox after analyzing a problem. The idea is that the analysis of emotional events should be conscious and not intuitive.

In the example of Michelle and the unhelpful clerk, Michelle spotted that she could yell at the clerk or act indifferently to her. She spotted that she could tell friends about the incident all day long or remove it from her thoughts. Michelle spotted that the event was only a triviality. It was not dangerous.

With repetition and focus, a human develops insight into which tool applies to an event. The ultimate goal is to spot the tool that applies to a situation immediately. Low called this *trigger spotting.*[9]

This is only the goal. It isn't attainable at first. You should not become discouraged, if at first, you are not very adept at spotting. It can take time to break bad behavioral habits. Even with time a person will not be able to spot on every occasion. No one can practice perfectly. Sometimes others can assist us.

Spotting changes reactions to events. Eventually, the practice can apply to bigger issues. (Examples of events and the spotting techniques that apply are included on subsequent pages.)

"Whatever you can do, or dream you can, begin it. Boldness has genius, power and magic in it." Goethe, German author

"If you want a quality, act as if you already had it." William James, U.S. psychologist

THE ROLE OF WILL

A person can spot the techniques that apply to an emotional situation using perception and analysis. Actual implementation of the method requires the "**the will to effort**[10]." This is the most basic tool.

A student can learn the techniques in a week or two. It is a minor intellectual feat. However, knowing the system and actually practicing it are very different.

Healthy thinking and behavior often collide with the natural tendencies of a nervous person; say Fearful Fran or Angry Arnold, to seek comfort. They will feel temporary personal discomfort when they choose the healthy path. If Fearful Fran or Angry Arnold is tempted to avoid discomfort, he or she can use fortitude to insist on healthy thoughts and behavior.

An act of resoluteness can transcend past limitations to produce long-term growth. It can be painful, especially at first. Eventually, application of will creates greater ability to function.

Mental Health through Will Training includes the expression "commanding the muscles to do what you fear to do."[11]   That is the essence of using will power for self-leadership. A fitness guru and an athletic shoe company use another saying in regard to will: "Just do it."

"Man acts as though he were the shaper and master of language, while in fact language remains the master of man." Martin Heidegger, German philosopher

"...language, if used glibly, tends to be alarmist and defeatist." Abraham A. Low, M.D.[12]

"AVOID TEMPERAMENTAL LINGO"[13]

Many people are too emotional. They often seek excitement, stimulation and a sense of drama. The Recovery theory is that people use exaggerated language to magnify their feelings. A good experience is the "greatest ever." A recurring pain is unbearable or "the worst ever experienced." In addition, profanity and vulgarity seem to have increased over the years.

The use of intemperate language is a habit that develops over years. The result is chronic self-excitation. The effect of language is especially strong on sensitive individuals who may be unusually suggestible.

Examples of temperamental language:

"That's incredible!"

"That's amazing!"

"It's mind-boggling!"

"Unbelievable!"

"Wow!"

"I detest him!"

"You idiot!"

"I botched the job!"

"That's awful!"

"That's a **BIG** decision."

"I have unbearable tenseness."

***

To improve health, avoid exaggerated language that inflames. A human can increase stability by using neutral language, instead. (An example is the term depression. Abraham Low believed the word itself was depressing. He required his patients to use the expression "lowered feelings.[14]" Low attributed these ideas about language to the semanticist Alfred Korzybski.) Some argue that the use of exciting language provides color and stimulation. Realistically, health is more important.

By controlling temperamental language, you enhance your objectivity, tranquility and realism. Language provides an opportunity to work on health.

"Each bird loves to hear himself sing." Arapaho proverb

"Silence is a true friend who never betrays" Confucius

"TO TALK IT UP IS TO WORK IT UP"[15]

This tool reflects Low's concept of "**processing**[16]."
Angry Arnold relates an upsetting event to friends, relatives
and acquaintances. He becomes upset when talking about the
situation. He begins to calm down. Then he tells others
about the everyday event and becomes excited again with
each retelling. This is processing.

The inclination to talk about situations that excite has the
effect of increasing self-arousal. Each retelling returns focus
to the event and forgetting about the event is difficult in that
scenario. Instead, each mention reminds Arnold of the upset
or perceived injustice. As long as he remembers he will
discuss the situation. It is a cycle that can over-stimulate.

Self-leadership requires that we limit our processing. We
can refuse to talk or dwell on minor upsetting events
repeatedly. The effort can be difficult because processing is
exciting and dramatic. We should care enough about health
to give up some excitement.

The result of the effort is that we forget about upsetting
events much sooner. Self-excitation is lower and we become
tranquil sooner. We maintain our calm, which allows us to
see other events with better perspective and clarity.

The effort to control processing is uncomfortable at first.
The long-term result, however, is greater tranquility.

"You must learn to be still in the midst of activity and be vibrantly alive in repose." Indira Gandhi, Indian Prime Minister

"CALM BEGETS CALM, TEMPER BEGETS TEMPER."[17]

A body in motion tends to stay in motion. This is a law of physics. A similar law applies to emotions. A person who tends to excite himself will tend to stay excited and tense. Tenseness destabilizes. On the other hand, the soul who achieves tranquility tends to remain tranquil.

The natural tendency for many people is to savor the stimulation of excitement. Unfortunately, the person who has become excited will likely become more upset when confronted with a second frustration. The calmer person, conversely, does not become upset so easily. The calm human is most likely to remain composed.

Judging, insecurity and self-importance may produce temper. Being group-minded, non-judgmental and realistic encourages tranquility. Remaining calm leads to more tranquility. Temper produces tenseness which leads to more temper. Our philosophy can determine whether we become calm or not.

"How many therapists does it take to change a light bulb? One, but the light has to want to change."

"Common sense and a sense of humor are the same thing, moving at different speeds. A sense of humor is just common sense, dancing."
William James, U.S. philosopher

"Be careful reading health books. You may die of a misprint." Mark Twain

"HUMOR IS OUR BEST FRIEND, TEMPER OUR WORST ENEMY"[18]

Unfortunately, serious people often have an unhealthy tendency to avoid the humor in life. The tense person does not always see the humor in situations and a lack of humor can contribute to tenseness. It is a vicious cycle. Appreciating funny things helps to break this cycle.

Humor is relaxing as it is hard to be angry when laughing. Humor also helps you see the big picture and maintain perspective. Scientific studies have proven that humor is good for your physical and mental health.

A human mind can only hold one thought at a time. If you are angry, you think about who is right and who is wrong. While angry, you cannot simultaneously think about what is ridiculous.

The converse is also true. When you are amused, you do not feel anger. You are not as likely to feel hate or insecurity while laughing. Since you can only focus on one thought, you are better off to make that one thought a humorous one. The tool is to encourage humor at the expense of temper.

Some people enjoy the comic pages of the daily newspaper. Others enjoy the Three Stooges, Little Rascals and the Marx Brothers. There are books and calendars of cartoons. There are great cartoons in magazines such as *The New Yorker*. A number of feature comedies appear at the movies each year. Television offers situation comedies and cartoons most nights. Large cities have comedy nightclubs. Cable has a comedy channel. There are jokes on the internet.

Humor should be a basic part of life, not something unusual. Not everybody can be a stand-up comedian in Las Vegas but everyone has an opportunity to use humor. The tool is to embrace humor rather than to avoid or ignore it. This can displace temper and make life more enjoyable.

"'Blessed is the man who expects nothing, for he shall never be disappointed' was the ninth beatitude." Alexander Pope (1688-1744), English poet

"PREDISPOSE"[19]

Carlos knows his license plates are about to expire. He drives to the license bureau at noon and finds the agency's room is full of customers. Carlos becomes frustrated and angry. His transaction takes an hour to complete. The lines, the waiting and the forms irritate him.

Carlos could have experienced fewer symptoms if he had predisposed. He had been to the license bureau before and had faced similar situations.

To predispose is to anticipate the conditions that are going to exist in a situation and to anticipate the efforts needed to cope. Carlos could predispose that he would have to be patient with the bureau personnel and other customers. Carlos could predispose that he would bear discomfort. The hassle of the experience would not be a surprise.

Through predisposition we prepare for an unpleasant experience and lower our expectations. Therefore, we can begin our efforts before the unpleasant event actually begins. We can do our spotting ahead of time and determine which tools will apply. As a result, our symptoms are less severe.

Low's writings emphasize the desirability of preparing for partnership and self-leadership.

"Selfishness is not living as one wishes to live; it is asking others to live as one wishes to live." Oscar Wilde

"He that would live in peace and at ease, must not speak all he knows nor judge all he sees." Benjamin Franklin

"There will be trouble if the cobbler starts making pies." Russian proverb

"REALISM AND ROMANTICISM"[20]

Romanticism involves the special, the unusual. Far away places, daring feats and extraordinary achievements are romantic. Many of us possess romantic ideas.

An intellectual feeling that creates problems is the perception of unusual ability to see what is best in situations. Low called this "**the vanity of knowing better**.[21]" The intellectualist feels other people do not share his ability. The romantic propensity of such a person is to share this special insight and to direct others.

There are several consequences to such thinking and behavior. Many individuals do not want advice from others. Such people have their own vanity about what is best and they resent unsolicited guidance. The romantic, on the other hand, often feels insulted when his or her advice is rejected and the emotions in such situations run deep.

What, then, should you do for health? You should embrace realism, the idea that other people are capable of directing their own affairs. In addition, a person has only a limited ability to see what is right and optimal. Understand that other people have pride about their own insight. You benefit by recognizing that other people's problems are not necessarily your responsibility. Others are responsible for their own decisions and the results of those decisions.

The effort should be to fight the inclination to guide. If advice is ignored, accept this as a typical human response. An individual develops personal humility as opposed to vanity when refusing to direct others. The result is improved health and relationships. It's a matter of will and practice to let others decide for themselves.

"What the world needs is more geniuses with humility, there are so few of us left."   Oscar Levant

"Self-endorsement is so important because the sense of security which it produces makes for sure and determined action." Abraham A. Low, M.D.[22]

"ENDORSE FOR THE EFFORT"[23]

Many individuals expect to perform at a high level and are hard on themselves. When such people don't excel they experience self-criticism and self-distrust. Such thinking becomes a habit.

Self-criticism over time produces low self-esteem. The antidote to low self-esteem is self-congratulation. Abraham Low called this **"endorsement."** Each time you try to think or act in a healthy way, endorse. Endorsement can be a mental note of self-congratulation or it could be a physical pat on the back or an ice cream sundae.

When you try to be group-minded, you should endorse. When you excuse someone, you should endorse. When you bear discomfort to accomplish a task, you should endorse for the endeavor. When you embrace secure thoughts, endorse.

RICK'S COMMENT: I have had trouble endorsing. I was waiting for perfect results before I congratulated myself. As a perfectionist, I found it hard to endorse unless my practice led to a perfect outcome. The tool works if you endorse for the effort made. Endorse for the effort and the results will follow. An attempt made to improve health is enough to earn endorsement.

***

Self-endorsement does not come easily. It takes a lot of practice before it becomes automatic.

On a job you expect payment. When you work for health your payment is endorsement. It is the paycheck for effort made.

PART 2.   GROUP FOCUS

"Egotist: A person of low taste, more interested in himself than in me." Ambrose Bierce (1842-1914)

"Genius is the capacity for seeing relationships where lesser men see none."
William James, U.S. psychologist and philosopher

"BE GROUP-MINDED NOT SELF-MINDED"[24]

Self-focus detracts from health. The words all have a negative connotation: self-centered, egotistical, egocentric, selfish, a loner, standoffish, unfriendly, and antisocial. The words have a bad reputation because almost all doctors and therapists recognize that being too self-centered is a risk to mental health.

When self-minded, we feel important. We are concerned with our pride, vanity, status, control of others, and power in relation to others. We may consider our own feelings exclusively. Typically, the egocentric do not have symptoms worrying too much about others. Fear and anxiety are usually self-centered. In addition, self-importance and vanity can lead to anger. An individual can lose sight of the big picture when he thinks only about himself/herself.

Being group-minded takes us away from selfish thinking and behavior. The group could be family, a work group, a religious community, a neighborhood or even society as a whole. Each group has its own purpose. It is healthy for us to support the purpose of most groups.

There are fraternal, social, spiritual, professional and civic groups we can join. By joining a group or volunteering to help others, we move away from selfishness. Feeling a part of a group and supporting its goals can eventually improve health.

For a family group, we should try to contribute to peace and harmony. Avoid fighting. Being group-minded requires cutting the others in the group some slack. At work, its best to see what our co-workers are trying to accomplish and to see the point-of-view of our boss and the other workers. Getting along with others is a long-term proposition that benefits from our flexibility.

Being group-minded can lower anxiety and help us maintain a total view. Are we group-minded to help others? Partially. Mainly, we are group-minded to help ourselves. We work on being group oriented by being considerate and supportive of others. The result of the effort is that our relationships with others improve. The group benefits and so do we.

"Be silent as to services you have rendered, but speak of favors you have received." Seneca (5 B.C.-65A.D)

SERVICE AND DOMINATION[25]

ROSINA'S COMMENT: I have a daughter that I raise myself. I have always guided her to keep her out of trouble. I would tell her what to do and how to act. What I finally realized is that I was using my guidance as a way to dominate my daughter. My focus developed, over time, towards dominating my daughter and not on helping her.

***

There are many occasions when individuals choose between service and domination. The healthy choice is usually service to another individual or group. The choice of domination is a common tendency that generates self-excitation and poisons relationships.

It is a good idea to reflect on service to others. Does the service include domination of the one being helped? Group orientation thrives on service to others, not on domination.

PART 3. MUSCLE CONTROL AND WILL

"Do every day or two something for no other reason than you would rather not do it, so that when the hour of dire need draws nigh, it may find you not unnerved and untrained to stand the test."   William James

"MUSCLE CONTROL"[26]

Many of us have fears that limit daily actions. Some of us are afraid to go shopping. Some may be afraid to apply for a new job or talk to the boss. There are people afraid to drive a car.

We can overcome fears by commanding our muscles. Maria, for example, had a fear of crowds. Because of this, she avoided crowds and her fear intensified. Using the Recovery tool, she overcame her fear to some extent and functioned in spite of her fear.

MARIA'S COMMENT: I commanded my muscles to walk into a crowd at the mall. I learned from the experience that the action I took did not harm me. I did not die. I didn't collapse. I realized there was no danger. However, I did feel symptoms. I went back to the mall another day and walked. I did not want to walk but commanded my muscles to walk at the mall. Eventually, my fear decreased.

***

The action Maria took was muscular in nature. Moving her muscles was also an act of will. A person can also command muscles not to move at all or to move slowly.

When she commanded her muscles to do something Maria learned from the experience. Abraham Low expressed the idea that the accomplishments and experiences our muscles produce re-educate the brain[27]. Our muscular action teaches that we are able to accomplish many tasks we are afraid to try. Our muscle action-which requires will-becomes our teacher[28].

Recovery uses the term *"move your muscles"* in another sense. Symptoms can become a focal point. People dwell on fear or anger. Often they are too upset to take action and only think instead about what is upsetting.

A way to break this cycle is to move the muscles. We can walk, exercise, clean or work on a project. Such action displaces the unhealthy thoughts from our minds and can objectify our thoughts. We thus change our focus to the task we face. (Another mental health saying: Keep your mind where your feet are.)

We control muscles for two different reasons. The first is an act of self-control to overcome fear or anger. The second reason is to keep busy in order to alter thoughts away from symptoms.

"Half our life is spent trying to find something to do with the time we have rushed through life trying to save." Will Rogers

"DON'T RUSH"[29]

This tool is not mentioned often at Recovery meetings in this form. But it was a concept Low wrote about. The idea is that rushing generates tenseness and a lack of tranquility.

A person may rush because of insecurity or an exaggerated sense of responsibility. There are tools for such symptoms.

The 12 step programs use the phrase *Easy Does It* that suggests the same concept. You can enhance the sense of calm and tranquility by not rushing. It is a matter of muscle control to slow down.

"By commanding your muscles to move you had transformed *the vicious cycle of helplessness* into the *vitalizing cycle of self-confidence*." Abraham A. Low, M.D.[30]

"VICIOUS CYCLES AND VITALIZING CYCLES"[31]

What is the "vicious cycle?" The idea is that temper, either angry or fearful, can produce tenseness. In turn, a tense feeling can predispose a human being to more temper and insecurity. As a result, a person feels incapable of moving the muscles to perform a task. The result is a type of paralysis in which the person cannot perform.

The "vitalizing cycle" refers to embracing group focus and security in order to act. With less tension, the body can relax and perform tasks with more confidence. By moving muscles and performing a task, the mind sees that the situation is not hopeless and the paralysis is broken.

David D. Burns, in *Feeling Good*, says a false supposition is that motivation always precedes action. Burns says this is false. Action can generate motivation. The motivation, in turn, generates further action.

PART 4. FEAR AND ANXIETY MANAGEMENT

"The perfect is the enemy of the good." Voltaire

"Be not ashamed of mistakes and thus make them crimes."
Confucius

"You have no idea what a poor opinion I have of myself and
how little I deserve it." W.S. Gilbert (1836-1922), English
librettist, in *Ruddigore*

PERFECTIONISM AND ONESELF

Sensitive people create symptoms by expecting too much
from themselves. Some see perfectionism as a virtue. In
reality, it can be a cross to bear. A popular term to describe
the perfectionist is to use the label high-strung.
Abraham Low called his idea of perfectionism
"exceptionality."[32] The model was that a nervous person
usually anticipated performing at an exceptional level. The
concept stressed self-importance added to perfectionism.
With exceptionality, failure to perform at the highest level
produces anger directed inward. The perfectionist has no
margin for error. A tennis player hits a shot into the net and
throws his racket in frustration. A diner drops a dinner
utensil and swears at herself. A baseball player strikes out
and breaks his bat in disgust.
The solution to perfectionism of this sort is to expect less
of ourselves. Realistic standards produce less frustration and
anger. According to psychologist Albert Ellis, many of us
have all or nothing feelings: we feel we are either perfect or

worthless.

Low called his solution **"averageness"**[33], the idea being that we each have an average level of performance that is less than perfection. Dr. Low mentioned *"good, plain and poor average"* in one book[34]. The idea is not to advocate mediocrity, but to learn to accept some imperfection. Actually, many average people are successful and happy. Most perfectionists are not as happy.

Additionally, people who insist on perfection can be less efficient. Failure to be perfect generates frustration and tenseness. Edginess in turn often causes mistakes. The situation can create a negative cycle that can substantially lower personal performance.

Our performance tends to be optimal when we try to do a good job while accepting some imperfection. We are more relaxed, more flexible and less likely to make mistakes. Most of us do not have to worry about trying to excel. We have to worry about expecting to be perfect.

"My apprehensions come in crowds,
I dread the rustling of the grass;
The very shadows of the clouds
Have power to shake me as they pass:
I question things and do not find
One that will answer to my mind;
And all the world appears unkind."
Wordsworth, English poet

"Some of the worst things that ever happened to me never happened." Mark Twain, U.S. author

"REPLACE INSECURE THOUGHTS WITH SECURE THOUGHTS"[35] *

JAMAL'S' COMMENT: I have had racing thoughts. These incessant worries and negative thoughts gave me no rest. They would come rapidly. Sometimes it seemed they would never stop.

As I learned the Recovery Method at self-help meetings, I found that I could replace insecure thoughts with secure thoughts. As an example, I had a fear that I would lose my job because of depression. That was an insecure thought that hounded me. It was something I thought about a lot.

When I first had the apprehension, I had nothing to fight it with. Today I can replace the thought with several secure thoughts: (1) my company seldom fires anyone, (2) I might qualify for a pension, (3) I have personal savings that would help, (4) I have already worked for my company successfully for many years and (5) I have job talents other employers could use.

When I began to use this tool, it took me a while to find secure thoughts. And after I thought of a secure idea, the insecure thought returned. I became discouraged.

The leader of the group I attended mentioned that if the insecure thought returns, keep replacing it with a secure thought. Eventually it helped.

At meetings, I heard the others use the tool successfully and I began to use it myself. With many reps, it began to help.

A way to use the tool as a project, I found, is to list secure thoughts on a notebook paper. I list things like work skills, friends and insurance programs. I revue the list at times and I try to add to it.

***

Insecure thoughts can be a symptom of several nervous and psychological disorders. Doctors sometimes prescribe treatments that help with some of these conditions. Jamal was somewhat aware of insecure thoughts, for example, even with treatment. (The program doesn't offer advice regarding medicine. That is a matter between the person and his or her health provider.)

A common insecure feeling is that a recurring worry won't end. The secure thought is that symptoms have a limited duration. Another source of security is that assistance is available to us. There are many doctors and therapists. We may have family or friends. New therapies are created periodically. There are non-profit agencies in many communities that provide help. There are support groups such as Recovery International in many cities or on the internet. We have resources.

(* A newer exposure therapy for OCD and other anxiety disorders uses a technique where intrusive thoughts are repeated until they are ignored.*)

"Pain makes men think.
Thinking gives man wisdom;
And wisdom confers peace."
Boris Pasternak, Russian author

"SYMPTOMS ARE DISTRESSING BUT NOT DANGEROUS"[36]

ALAN'S COMMENT: Before I learned the Recovery Method, I felt insecure and was plagued with an overactive imagination. I felt a sense of danger when I had a panic attack. My symptoms included racing thoughts and sweating. At times, I questioned my stability. I imagined the worst possible outcome when I looked into the future. When I described my symptoms, I used temperamental language to inflame my emotions.

Then I learned that *"symptoms are distressing but not dangerous."* Blushing and perspiration are anxiety symptoms that do not harm me. Distressing sensations did not permanently damage me. By embracing security, I learned to "*take the danger out of my symptoms.*[37]"

***

Someone at a Recovery meeting said that no one ever died from a nervous symptom. This is probably true but the idea is sometimes forgotten when it is needed most. You can take the danger out of your symptoms by embracing security. In using the tool, you are replacing thoughts of danger with thoughts of safety to control imagination.

"Of all the passions, fear weakens judgment most." Cardinal de Retz, (1614-1679), *Memoirs*

"Do not anticipate trouble, or worry about what may never happen. Keep in the sunlight." Benjamin Franklin

"POSSIBILITIES AND PROBABILITIES"[38]

Humans often imagine that bad things will happen. They often predict catastrophe when looking into the future.

Abraham Low suggested that the way to analyze insecurity is to ask whether the scenario is a possibility, a probability or a certainty.

Sensitive Sue had insecure thoughts that her car would fail. Analyzing the situation, Sue could see that the car breakdown was not a certainty. Furthermore, she saw that the failure was only a remote possibility. The probability was that the car would run for a long time.

After analyzing her situation, Sue felt greater security. She had consciously worked to relieve her fearful temper.

"The quality of decision is like the well-timed swoop of a falcon which enables it to strike and destroy its victim." Sun Tzu, *The Art of War*

"Anyone who has never made a mistake has never tried anything new." Albert Einstein

"Even if you're on the right track, you'll get run over if you just sit there." Will Rogers

"MAKE A DECISION AND STICK TO IT"[39]

DON'S COMMENT: The rubber molding was separating from my car in a spot. I ignored it and a few months later it was worse. I couldn't decide whether to take it in to the dealership for repair or fix it myself. I am cheap and have had some expensive surprises at the dealership. The car is not under warranty.

I thought about the expense of a dealership repair. On the other hand, I wasn't sure I could fix the problem well. It wasn't really an important decision, but it bothered me quite a bit.

I thought about the situation for about a week. Then I made a decision. I decided to buy some adhesive and fix it myself.

As soon as I made the decision I felt much better. Before Recovery I would have agonized over the decision for weeks.

***

Until Don decided what to do, he was inundated by insecure thoughts. The difficulty of making a decision occupied his mind. He thought about the possibility and consequences of making a bad decision.

The outcome of such thinking can be paralysis-an inability to decide. The way to break such a cycle is to make a decision. You could make a mistake in deciding and acting. What Recovery recommends is the **"courage to make a mistake**[40].**"** The effort is to make a decision even if you risk making an error.

Because of high expectations you may want to make a perfect decision. This can cause you to agonize about your choices and procrastinate. Constant focus, analysis and speculation only end when you make a decision.

Rather than procrastinate, you should lower your standards and hope for the best. The goal should not be a perfect decision with a perfect outcome. A body has to be able to accept imperfection and understand that life is not always ideal. There is not a perfect solution for every problem.

To make decisions requires resolve, the courage to risk making a mistake and control of perfectionism. The reward is less anxiety and more tranquility.

"The man with insight enough to admit his limitations comes nearest to perfection." Goethe, German author

"DROP THE 'EXAGGERATED SENSE OF RESPONSIBILITY'"[41]

You read in newspapers about problems that are caused by people who do not take responsibility for their actions. It is quite common. For many anxiety patients, ironically, the problem is often the opposite. A large number have an *exaggerated sense of responsibility*.

At work, such an employee may try too hard to excel, focusing on personal production. An anxious person can feel responsible for the success of an entire group or organization. Some people constantly try to prove their worthiness.

The real responsibility should be to take care of your own affairs and health. An exaggerated feeling of responsibility can enlarge the area of things to worry about. It opens new concerns that produce symptoms.

It's important to realize that others are responsible and can contribute. In groups, other people may be able to produce results. Before assuming ownership, examine situations with that perspective. Dropping the exaggerated sense of responsibility can lead to greater calm.

"The ultimate umpire of all things in life is fact." Agnes Laut, (1871-1936), Canadian author

"FEELINGS ARE NOT FACTS"[42]

JEFF'S COMMENT: I stood in line at the store. It was late spring and I wore shorts. However, it turned unseasonably cool that afternoon. I noticed that everyone else was wearing long pants. I had a feeling inside that everyone was aware of me because of the shorts; that I stood out by wearing something inappropriate.

Then I remembered the tools. I spotted that *"feelings are not facts."* The feeling was the product of an overactive imagination. My personal insecurity and suggestibility combined to produce a feeling. This was not supported by any data or facts. It was only a feeling. It was possible the feeling was bogus.

***

Many people with active imaginations experience a number of strange feelings. Jeff was better off to discount such feelings and to recognize that they are temporary notions. Unless there are facts to support it, dismiss some feelings as unimportant and baseless.

"Most of the important things in the world have been accomplished by people who have kept on trying where there seemed to be no hope at all." Dale Carnegie

"NO HOPELESS CASES"[43]

LINDA'S COMMENT: When I first had lowered feelings I felt that my situation was hopeless. I experienced incessant negative thoughts. My future seemed bleak.

I worked with a doctor who helped me. I attended Recovery meetings. My condition slowly improved. My thoughts eventually became more secure. I tried to become more group-minded. I learned the tools and learned to control my perfectionism. I was making progress. My situation was no longer hopeless.

***

The experience of many others is similar to that of Linda. New people, some after a setback, come to the Recovery Method with a sense of hopelessness. The new people see others doing well and can't relate at first. Eventually they talk to others who have recovered. The common experience is that setbacks are not permanent.

Eventually most sufferers improve. Doctors provide treatments that help. The support of family and friends helps. The fellowship of others at support groups helps and determined effort to apply Recovery tools will eventually pay off.

Many cases seem hopeless at first. But the individual can't always make such a prediction. Only the health professional is qualified to make a prognosis. Seeing the possibility of improvement is an important step.

"One never notices what has been done; one can only see what remains to be done." Marie Curie, scientist

DISCOUNTING THE POSITIVE[44]

Some people are so insecure and negative that they have difficulty expressing a positive statement.

WILMA: "I got a promotion but I don't think it will last."
JUAN: "I got straight A's this semester but I don't think I can do it again."
ANN: "I feel better but I think it's only temporary."

The word "but" is used to discount the positive in these statements. Abraham Low coined the term "butknocking[45]" to describe the technique.

To be self-led, accept improvement without adding a qualification every time. Rather than adding insecurity and negativity to comments, endorse for the efforts that led to improvement.

"We gain the strength of the temptation we resist." Ralph Waldo Emerson, *Essays: First Series*

"Fall down seven times, get up eight." Japanese proverb

"RETURN OF THE SYMPTOM IS NOT THE RETURN OF THE ILLNESS"[46]

A person who has had a setback or experienced a psychological illness doesn't soon forget. Such an individual will naturally fear a setback.

Everyday symptoms of discomfort and annoyance are similar to those felt during a setback. It is a matter of degree. The thing to remember is that feelings of discomfort, anger or sadness do not necessarily indicate a major relapse. Symptoms are ever-present.

Understand that a symptom, even if a strong one, is not proof of a major setback. It is usually just a part of everyday stress. Patients can work against a setback by working with a health professional. The Recovery tools and self-help meetings help. In most areas, there are organizations to help. There are support groups and forums on the Internet as well. When in doubt, one should accept the secure thought that the return of a symptom is most likely a temporary matter.

PART 5. ANGER MANAGEMENT

"It disturbs me no more to find men base, unjust, or selfish than to see apes mischievous, wolves savage, or the vulture ravenous for its prey." Moliere, French dramatist

PERFECTIONISM AND OTHERS

The perfectionist usually extends expectations of the ideal to others. This is the flip side of *exceptionality*. With pride in his ability, the perfectionist anticipates being treated with the deference and consideration that high ability merits. People do not usually treat any of us in such a special way. Routine treatment produces frustration and anger in the perfectionist.

As an example, Steve was busy as a computer operator. His work was piling up. The other operators had other responsibilities but few active tasks. Steve thought about the situation and became angry because no one offered to help him. In frustration, he kicked his desk and caused a scene.

In addition, Steve anticipated others performing without error. He was highly critical of imperfection in others he dealt with.

A Recovery tool that applies is to **"accept others at their own average."**[47] Employees in an organization do not typically offer to work outside their assigned duties. The lack of assistance was not unusual. It was Steve's ideal hope that was dysfunctional because he expected others to anticipate his needs and respond. Steve was also wrong when he expected flawlessness from others.

We should not transform preferences into expectations that others will behave the way we want. It is not realistic or helpful. We can also learn to expect that others will be oblivious to our wants. Other people do not spend much time, if any, anticipating our desires.

Steve believed that the indifference of others caused his anger. Many of us go for years blaming others for our emotions. It is important to realize that we create our own emotions based on assumptions. Anticipating indifference and imperfection from others is a very important technique in anger management.

"Nothing is so good as it seems beforehand." George Eliot, *Silas Marner*

"The rain falls on the just and the unjust." Hopi proverb

"EXPECT FRUSTRATIONS"[48]
"SELF-APPOINTED EXPECTATIONS LEAD TO SELF-INDUCED FRUSTRATIONS"[49]

Juan applied for a corporate job. The personnel office told him that his chances were very good. Two weeks later the company announced an accounting problem and filed for bankruptcy.

Juan had expected to obtain a good job. Instead, he had to apply for other jobs. Juan felt anger and disappointment.

The point to note is that the disappointment did not solely create Juan's anger. A lofty expectation made his anger and frustration that much stronger. By anticipating less, Juan's anger would have been modest.   If he tempers his expectations, Juan is apt to have milder symptoms.

Abraham Low wrote that frustrations are a frequent part of everyone's life. By anticipating frustrations, people are realistic and not as frequently disappointed or surprised.

Another pertinent tool: **"the outer environment can be rude, crude and indifferent[50]."** The outer environment can include people, organizations and even machines. The realistic thought is that the outer environment is usually uninterested in our wishes. Over time, we can train ourselves to expect less. With lower assumptions we become less excitable.

"One often contradicts an opinion when what is uncongenial is really the tone in which it was conveyed." Friedrich Nietzsche, German philosopher

"The art of being wise is the art of knowing what to overlook." William James, U.S. psychologist and philosopher

"CHOOSE PEACE OVER POWER"[51]

To Edgy Ellen, prevailing in a disagreement was the same as being worthwhile. She experienced an opposing view as a **"threat to one's personality**[52]**."** Losing an argument threatened her self-esteem.

Ellen's natural inclination was to argue as a point of pride. Again, in Recovery language, this is the quest for the "*symbolic victory*." Ellen improved her health by dropping her efforts to prove other people wrong. Peace with others requires group focus and a sense of fellowship. Power involves personal authority and victory over others.

ELLEN'S COMMENT: I have a history of losing my temper in disagreements with others. At work, I would yell when assistants made a mistake. I would jump on them hard. I chose power over peace.

At home, my husband and I would argue about sharing the house cleaning. The disagreements I had with my husband and others were long-standing.

At a support group people talked about disagreements and I was surprised how small topics create big arguments. Then

I reconsidered my own arguments. My power struggles with my husband were often about washing the dishes. I could see absurdity in the arguments of others but lost perspective in my own life.

I didn't want to give up my tendency to condemn those who oppose me. I eventually tried choosing *"peace over power."* When I decided to cut others slack I felt better. I maintained my composure better. I learned it was a choice I could make.

***

Ellen improved her tranquility, composure, perspective and objectivity by avoiding strife. This is a high form of self-leadership.

By arguing less, long-term relationships improve. People who know they could upset Ellen are less likely to try when she learns to avoid arguments. People are less likely to *"push her buttons."* Friends and family become less defensive when they do not expect a fight because each individual invests less pride in his or her point of view. The result is less discord.

A similar concept involves fellowship and sovereignty[53]. The tool is to **choose fellowship over sovereignty**, stressing group membership over individual power.

After her disagreements, Ellen would seethe for hours and lose sleep. She would talk about arguments and relive the excitement they created. Ellen remained tense and small disappointments upset her further. By choosing "peace over power," Ellen became less symptomatic and her relationships improved.

"All human knowledge takes the form of interpretation."
Walter Benjamin, (1892-1940), German critic

"Never attribute to malice that which is adequately explained
by stupidity." William James, U.S. psychologist and
philosopher

"PEOPLE DO THINGS THAT IRRITATE US, NOT ALWAYS TO IRRITATE US"[54]

Angry Arnold has the unhealthy tendency to assume that
intentional actions usually create frustrations. People often
do things that bother him.   He errs when he always assumes
such actions are intentional. The assumption of malice and
the anger that results occur instantly and without reflection.
Effective anger management depends on replacing this
unhealthy assumption.

The human tendency is to want to find someone to blame
for every bad thing that happens. This is irrational. The
inclination does not usually help. We cannot read the minds
of other people although that is the natural expectation of
sensitive people. In these situations, our imaginations guide
us in the wrong direction.

As an example, Arnold is standing on a bus. When the
bus comes to a sudden stop, another rider loses balance and
steps on Arnold's toe. Arnold instantly blames the other bus
rider for the incident. Actually, it was nothing personal at all.
The other bus rider did not plan to step on anyone's toe.

Certainly, there are times when people intentionally
irritate us. Nevertheless, if there is any doubt at all we

should not assume malice. Life is better when we see that not every discomfort is intentional. If we practice this tool religiously, it may eventually become an automatic response. It requires time and repetition. If a new philosophy develops, we conquer an unhealthy way of thinking.

"A person is only as big as the things that make him angry."
Confucius

"TEMPER BLOCKS INSIGHT"[55]

CHUCK'S COMMENT: I was in line at a fast food
restaurant on my break from work. The lady ahead of me
made a big order that slowed my line. The lines on both
sides of me moved fast. I got heated as I waited for my line
to move. When I finally got to the clerk, I ordered the wrong
item by mistake and became more upset.

At the time, I was angry with the customer with the large
order and the clerk for the delay. In hindsight, I see that the
delay was only a matter of chance. I really had no reason to
be mad at either person.

***

Chuck's temper affected his composure and ability to
think clearly. Chuck was so upset he ordered something
from the menu he had not wanted. Additionally, he took his
wait in line personally and blamed others when no one had
erred.

Chuck anticipated he could buy his meal quickly. At
lunchtime, this is not always realistic. If Chuck had lower
expectations, he would have had milder temper. If he had
excused the others, he would have had milder anger. With
less angry temper, Chuck may have performed at a higher
level and been able to concentrate better. With less temper,
he would have had more insight.

"Have you ever noticed? Anybody going slower than you is
an idiot, and anyone going faster than you is a maniac?"
George Carlin

"One who cannot dance blames the floor." Proverb of India

"EXCUSE RATHER THAN ACCUSE[56]"

Another unhealthy behavior is the tendency to indict. We
criticize ourselves when we err. We accuse others when they
slip up. Judgmental thinking generates hostility and anger
that lingers. In addiction, anger is a powerful stressor.

We often judge ourselves as harshly as we judge other
people. Accusing ourselves lowers our self-esteem while
excusing ourselves lowers our frustration and boosts
confidence.

The habit of criticism is inherent in some personalities and
it is difficult to break. Our parents may even have acted
critically when we were young. However, even long-term
habits can be changed. Each of us has the ability to think and
the strength to act. People tend to accuse automatically after
seeing a mistake. Afterward they can learn to excuse. With
effort, the excusing occurs sooner and the accusing is milder.

Excusing uses group-minded thinking and it limits
egocentricity. What's more, excusing requires a feeling of
partnership with others. Many spiritual traditions discourage
judgmental thinking to achieve spiritual growth. The idea is
ancient.

One way to remind ourselves to practice is by attending
self-help meetings such as those of Recovery International.
The techniques are mentioned at every meeting. Repetition

and practice create ability in the technique.

Our efforts should be in finding virtues. Alcoholics Anonymous uses the phrase "look for the good." Through finding virtues and good intentions, we will be less judgmental. If virtue isn't seen at first we should look again. Then we should often be able to excuse.

"Boldness, without the rules of propriety, becomes insubordination." Confucius

"ASSERT YOURSELF WITHOUT AGGRESSION"[57]

LISA'S COMMENT: I have an anxiety condition and tend to be very introverted. Because of my shyness, I have always been hesitant to assert myself with others.

What often happened is that I would not assert myself in important situations. When the situation became untenable, I would assert myself by exploding at someone else. This was usually embarrassing. In my mind, I conceived of assertion as snapping at someone to get my way. I went from one extreme to the other.

I learned from Recovery meetings, as well as a class I took at work, how to assert myself diplomatically. The idea is to feel free to assert yourself as long as you are not rude. Rather than waiting, I try to assert myself as soon as necessary. In that way, my situations are less likely to turn into upsetting emergencies.

I usually receive what I am due by using courtesy when I assert myself. I stay calmer and the people who deal with me stay calmer. The tool is difficult to adopt but helps me greatly.

***

Lisa's example is a common one. Lisa was reluctant to assert herself for fear of offending others. When she did finally assert herself, she was too aggressive. Lisa learned to assert herself in a timely way without aggression. It was difficult to accomplish but improved her ability to function.

"We must be as courteous to a man as we are to a picture, which we are willing to give the advantage of a good light." Ralph Waldo Emerson

"Those who in quarrels interpose,
  Must often wipe a bloody nose."   John Gay (1685-1732)

"ACT WITH CULTURE" "CULTURE WILL CURE US"[58]

Who isn't tempted to make rude remarks? Just about everyone is at some point in time. This is a tendency many frustrated people have. The average person can make a rude remark without much aftereffect. The sensitive soul feels regret and fearful temper after making a rude comment.

First, discourtesy is a sabotage of mental health. Self-leadership stresses group focus, peace and tranquility. Rudeness, snide remarks or angry outbursts are the antithesis of self-leadership. By consistently acting in a civil way we eventually lose the inclination to make cutting remarks. Such remarks inflame emotions. The effect of discourtesy is to allow anger to linger in our thoughts. Discourteous behavior can also produce regret that can last for many hours.

The other negative aspect of incivility is that it can alienate somebody with whom we have to deal. When we disparage someone else, we put that human on the defensive. The person is likely to argue or counter attack. Each side in a disagreement becomes more subjective and less objective.

We defuse such situations by acting with culture and

diplomacy. We tend to stay calm. Those around us stay calm. Our long-term relationships improve. We act with civility to help ourselves as much as to help others.

"Most of us retain enough of the theological attitude to think that we are little gods." Oliver Wendell Holmes, *The Mind and Faith of Justice Holmes*

"LITERALISM"[59] AND PEDANTRY

"The TV set costs about $460.00," said Tim, a shopper.
"No, the TV is $459.95," said Mike, another shopper.

The difference between the two figures was insignificant. Yet Mike insisted on correcting Tim. This is an example of literalism. Another term might be pedantry. The idea is to offer a correction on a fact that is insignificantly imprecise, where such a correction doesn't help anyone.

Why was there a desire to dispute such a trivial difference? In part, it reflected the vanity of knowing better. The individual making a correction feels pride in superior knowledge. Only an exceptional person would notice such a difference.

The desire to find a right versus wrong issue is also a factor. Some people find excitement in right versus wrong issues, no matter how inconsequential. Some individuals are constantly looking to find imprecision to dispute.

To work toward health, do not correct others over trifling differences. If a possible misstatement is not important, don't mention it. This new behavior requires effort. The benefit of such an effort is greater humility and less self-excitation.

"In rage, it is notorious how we 'work ourselves up' to a climax by repeated outbreaks of expression. Refuse to express a passion, and it dies. Count ten before venting your anger, and its occasion seems ridiculous." William James, U.S. psychologist, philosopher

EXPRESSING TEMPER[60]

According to older theories, a person has two options when angry. Not expressing anger, according to these theories, is harmful. Expressing anger, some say, makes the anger disappear.

The problem is that many people habitually express anger without any loss of temper. There are people who explode in anger almost every day. The feeling of temper can be habitual even with its regular expression.

Abraham Low's idea, as well as those of later cognitive therapies, is that there is another way. Since our beliefs about events create temper, changing our thoughts can greatly reduce our anger. Changing our beliefs in this way is like turning down the heat on a teakettle.

A person can most likely control anger by thinking artfully in the first place. In addition, expressing an incompetent emotion avoids addressing flawed thinking. Reflecting on the appropriateness of thoughts produces better self-control. A big outburst delays self-reflection for hours. The Recovery Method encourages the expression of *feelings* in a calm manner without a lot of drama.

PART 6. COMFORT AND WILL

"There is no doubt that life is given us, not to be enjoyed, but to be overcome-to be got over." Arthur Schopenhauer, German philosopher

"THE WILL TO BEAR DISCOMFORT"[61]

When facing symptoms we tend to stop our activities in order to relieve discomfort. This is the natural inclination to try to escape pain. Abraham Low taught that we should continue our activities, in many cases, in spite of uneasiness. We should practice the tools of self-leadership even if temporary discomfort results.

For example, Fearful Fran hated standing in long lines at the grocery store. To avoid the discomfort she shopped late at night when lines were shortest. As a matter of will and self-leadership, she forced himself to shop an hour or two earlier. Fran learned she could handle the extra discomfort. The successful act of will dispelled some of her fear.

How much discomfort can we bear? A lot! One Recovery member stated that there is no limit to the discomfort a human can choose to bear. It is a matter of courage and determination. In addition, when we bear discomfort actual situations are not usually as painful as anticipated.

To bear discomfort voluntarily is an act of will that merits self-respect. Using will, we can function despite discomfort. This is the epitome of self-management.

"Had there been no difficulties and no thorns in the way, then man would have been in his primitive state and no progress made in civilization and mental culture." Anandabai Joshee, (1865-1887), Indian physician.

"COMFORT IS A WANT AND NOT A NEED"[62]

JOSE'S EXAMPLE: I'm a salesman. I was on my way to meet a customer when I got a flat tire. I was wearing a suit.

I felt anger and frustration. Instead of arriving on time, I would be late and possibly dirty.

I spotted that *"comfort is a want and not a need."* I remembered that the outer environment can be rude, crude and indifferent. I could function without comfort. Before I learned the Recovery Method, I would have been much more upset.

***

The idea that life should be comfortable is a modern one. For many thousands of years life was a struggle as people faced starvation, inclement weather, wild beasts and disease. Early ancestors worked long hours under difficult conditions to survive. People worried more about physical survival than social anxiety and minor injustices.

With modern inventions and improvements in the standard of living, our expectations changed. In wealthier nations, some of us no longer anticipate discomfort. The reality, however, is that frustration is still a big part of life.

When we study in school or work at a job, there are frustrations. Maintaining a home requires an effort. Working with others creates frustration. The natural tendency is to say that we can not endure discomfort. In reality, we can. The self-disciplined individual can accomplish a lot because he or she can endure discomfort. People achieve big accomplishments by enduring discomfort.

The goal should be to function even if we lack comfort. We can work, socialize and support group goals without comfort. It is a matter of will, self-leadership and realism.

"Lest he should wander irretrievably from the right path, he stands still." William Hazlitt (1778-1830), English Essayist.

"WE DO THINGS TO GET WELL; WE DON'T WAIT TO GET WELL TO DO THINGS."[63]

      Juanita feared meeting with groups of people. Rather than facing the fear, she avoided taking a class that would help her at work. The postponement of activities continued for many years and limited her career.

A central idea is that Juanita should not allow emotional symptoms to dictate her actions. She should not wait until symptoms stop before acting. If Juanita waits until there are no symptoms, she could wait forever.

Juanita learned to do things to get well and lived actively in spite of her symptoms. By choosing to take the class, she proved that she is able to function. Through activity, she changed her belief about what she was able to do. To wait until there is no discomfort can postpone healthy accomplishment for a very long time.

"The man who can drive himself further once the effort gets painful is the man who will win."   Roger Bannister, British runner

"The rain does not recognize anyone as a friend; it drenches all equally." African proverb

"WE CAN'T BE COMFORTABLE IN AN UNCOMFORTABLE SITUATION"[64]

You attend a speech. The speaker is boring and talks for a very long time. How do you feel comfortable about the situation? You should not expect to feel comfortable. You should accept symptoms as routine.

People naturally expect comfort. Discomfort can suggest that there is something wrong with a person. Symptoms in the face of unpleasant situations are natural and do not reflect on competency or effort. The realistic idea is that discomfort is appropriate in some situations.

"There are many paths to the top of the mountain, but the view is always the same." Chinese proverb

"IT'S NOT HOW WE FEEL, IT'S HOW WE FUNCTION"[65]

When an accountant does your taxes, do you care about his discomfort? Probably not. You are not especially concerned about how the accountant feels. You want to see results. The same model should apply to your own performance.

An unhealthy tendency is to choose comfort over utility. The result is milder symptoms and less functionality. If you avoid a person or activity to avoid symptoms, you limit your effectiveness.

You have a choice. You can choose comfort or you can choose to function at a higher level. The Recovery Method recommends choosing functionality over comfort. It is a difficult choice to make that requires will power. The reward is an improved ability to live successfully.

"Sure I am of this, that you have only to endure to conquer. You have only to persevere to save yourself." Winston Churchill, British statesman, author

"BRAVE, FACE, TOLERATE AND ENDURE"[66]

VERNA'S COMMENT: If I don't like my sister-in-law, I don't have very many options. I can tolerate her or avoid her. I will try to tolerate my sister-in-law. The discomfort of dealing with her is only temporary. I now know that I should endorse when I "brave, face, tolerate and endure" my symptoms.

***

Situations that create unease are always out there. In order to function at a high level, Verna must face such situations despite apprehension. After all, she can't run from symptom-producing situations forever. In order to function, she chooses to "brave, face, tolerate and endure."

Fears, anger and embarrassment are endurable. They don't last forever. While Verna braves such symptoms, she should endorse for the effort.

"My thoughts are my company; I can bring them together, select them, detain them, dismiss them." Walter Savage Landor, (1775-1864), *Imaginary Conversations*

"THOUGHTS AND IMPULSES CAN BE CONTROLLED; FEELINGS AND SENSATIONS MUST RUN THEIR COURSE"[67]

There are things we can control and those we can't. What can we control? We can largely control our thoughts. For example, we can change insecure thoughts to secure beliefs. We can control our impulses with firmness. We should be able to derive some security from the things we can control. Controlling thoughts and impulses produces better health.

Feelings and sensations we can't control. For example, if an event is embarrassing, we blush and feel some temper. We cannot control how long such feelings last. It is beyond our control except for the idea that the feeling subsides sooner if we do not think about it repeatedly. Feelings and sensations decline on their own. Frustration about our inability to control those symptoms doesn't help.

A secure thought is that feelings and sensations have a limited duration. They will not last forever.

PART 7.   SELF-LEADERSHIP

"There's only one corner of the universe you can be certain of improving, and that's your own self." Aldous Huxley, British author

"Do something every day that you don't want to do, this is the golden rule for acquiring the habit of doing your duty without pain." Mark Twain

"BE SELF-LED NOT SYMPTOM-LED"[68]

BOB'S COMMENT: At one time, I had a fear of crowds. I would plan my activities to avoid crowds. My symptoms dictated when I could conduct my business.

I also had a bad temper. When I got mad, I would sometimes make a scene. Later, I would have to deal with the person I got mad at. This was usually embarrassing.

Before I learned the tools, symptoms often limited what I was able to accomplish. There were many activities I was afraid to start. There were times I could not get along with people well enough to accomplish my goals.

Self-leadership has changed that. If there is something I want to do, I use determination to begin the task. I do not allow fears to dictate what I can or cannot do. I do not allow anger to disrupt my activities and relationships. I am self-led to control my anger and fears, using the Recovery tools.

***

The basic Recovery Method idea is that a human should use will-power to choose the action rather than allowing symptoms to dictate behavior. Bob learned the tools and is now in the driver's seat. His symptoms are no longer controlling his life. The symptoms he does have are less severe now and less limiting.

Reading about the tools is self-leadership. Attending group meetings is self-leadership. Spotting the tool that pertains to a situation and acting appropriately is behavioral self-leadership. To work effectively with someone who irritates us is self-leadership. The self-led person embraces secure thoughts.

Developing leadership is a long-term process. It requires effort. It can be uncomfortable. The benefits are significant and worth the effort. The alternative, which is to allow symptoms to guide us, doesn't work.

"Human beings, by changing the inner attitudes of their minds, can change the outer aspects of their lives." William James, U.S. psychologist and philosopher

"CONTROL THE INNER AND THE OUTER WILL ADJUST"[69]

The theory behind this tool is that the outer environment is often uncontrollable. Can we control our boss or relatives? No. We can't control a traffic jam at rush hour. The automobile driver in front of us will still start and stop. Our impatience and frustration do not help many situations we can't control. Feelings about a traffic jam are irrelevant to the highway flow and the only manageable thing in this situation is our attitude, the inner environment.

Belief about a situation is the inner environment, which we can control. The external situation eventually adjusts. We gain perspective when we separate our thoughts from the external things we can't control. Another tool that conveys a similar concept is: **If you can't change an event you can change your attitude towards it**[70]. We have a choice in regard to what attitude we adopt. The attitude we choose will determine the emotion we experience.

The tool applies to fearful situations as well. Sometimes we must change our inner beliefs in order to deal with fears. Fear creating events are not eternal.

The majority of outer events aren't important. The traffic bottleneck is temporary. Our irritation about traffic should be fleeting.

One school of therapy suggests that individuals fixate about the way things SHOULD or MUST be. Anger management requires that we do not upset ourselves over situations beyond our control. We cannot afford it. It is counter-productive.

The tool can have spiritual elements. A Zen master or guru meditates all day, training in control of the inner mind. There is a history of meditation done in many religions.

A key to success in controlling the inner environment is repetition of effort. Skill does not develop overnight. It takes time and discipline.

"He who conquers others is strong; he who conquers himself is mighty." Lao Tsu, *The Way of Life*

"EACH ACT OF SELF-CONTROL BUILDS SELF-RESPECT"[71]

Another idea of Low was that using will power to function in spite of symptoms produces self-respect. When controlling anger, you should respect the effort. When you think of others or work toward group goals, you should feel proud. You should endorse when recognizing imperfection as routine. When someone functions in spite of fear, he or she has performed commendably.

Acts of self-control for emotional health should be a source of pride, based on effort extended. When you choose healthy thought and behavior, you should feel pride.

"Success is not final, failure is not fatal: It is the courage to continue that counts."   Winston Churchill

"Courage is resistance to fear, mastery of fear-not absence of fear." Mark Twain

"DON'T TAKE THE BID FOR INSTANT RELIEF"[72]

SARAH'S COMMENT: I was at work and my boss asked me to speak to some co-workers the next day about a new procedure we are to use. I have a fear of speaking with others and anticipated the meeting with dread. The next morning when I got up, I thought about calling in sick. Then I remembered self-leadership. I decided that I would not take *the bid for instant relief.* I would not bail out. I decided I could bear some discomfort. I also thought that I could be group-minded to my boss and co-workers by going to work and participating. Before Recovery, I would have called in sick.

(The work session went well and I was glad it was done.)

***

Taking the bid for instant relief means we are unwilling to practice self-leadership if it causes discomfort. It is the natural inclination for most humans to move away from painful situations. Sometimes a healthy choice is to face a problem directly. We perform better and teach ourselves when facing discomfort in order to accomplish a goal.

"A journey of a thousand miles must begin with a single step." *Lao-Tsu, The Way of Lao-Tsu*

"USE PART ACTS"[73]

MAUREEN'S COMMENT: I was always very conscientious. When I faced a project, I would feel overwhelmed. The entire effort always seemed too formidable. If a task had ten steps, I would worry about all ten steps at the same time. I learned from the method that it is counter-productive to focus on a job in its entirety.

I discovered that *"part acts"* is the solution to such thinking. I learned to break a project into its component parts and focus on the first element only. In doing this, I greatly limit what I can worry about. The first step to accomplish is much less imposing and worrisome than the entire project. The insecure thoughts I feel about one element of a project are a small fraction of the insecure thoughts I feel about an entire job.

When I am done with the first step of a job, I can then focus on the next step. "One step at a time" or "first things first" are two sayings that express the same concept.

***

Most people driving from New York to Los Angeles consider local traffic first. The anxious man or woman will think about this as well as the road conditions on every road along the way. Moreover, until the task is completed, such insecure thoughts can recur. Rather than having one concern, the anxious person considers a multitude of insecure thoughts.

You can use part acts when traveling, organizing a group event, cleaning, repairing a machine, doing a project at work, cooking or just about anything else. If there are ten things to do this week, you can use part acts to accomplish one thing at a time. When confronted with too many things to do a person can get discouraged and quit. Using part acts, you are more likely to begin and complete projects.

Some organizations give workers a preprinted form called a "to-do list." On the form, the worker lists the tasks he or she should perform in order of importance. This is the essence of part acts.

When you work one step at a time you work more effectively and are more secure. You become calmer and more objective about challenges you face.

"Need teaches a plan." Irish proverb

"DECIDE, PLAN AND ACT."[74]

Members recite this tool at most Recovery meetings. The tool applies when someone faces a difficult undertaking.

In order to accomplish something, you have to first decide what to do. The next step is to plan the steps necessary to achieve the goal. Finally, you should actually begin the first step of the project.

It sounds like common sense. But anxiety and perfectionism can paralyze. The tool may really encompass three others tools. (1) Make a decision. (2) Use *"Part Acts"* to break the task down into its steps. (3) Have the *Will to Effort* to begin.

"Patience and tenacity of purpose are worth more than their weight of cleverness." Thomas Henry Huxley (1825-95), English biologist

"MAKE YOUR HEALTH A BUSINESS, NOT A GAME"[75]

MARGARITA'S COMMENT: Before I learned the Recovery Method, I put many things in life ahead of my health. Winning arguments came before my health. I thought about myself and did not consider the group.

I wanted to show others I was right. I had to be comfortable. I was rude to people I disagreed with. I would generally go out of my way to avoid any discomfort.

I used to say that I worked on my health. In fact, many of the things I did took me away from health. I did not consider my mental health ahead of other factors. What I have learned is that nothing is more important. Without my peace of mind, I don't have anything.

***

Margarita thought she wanted health. However, many of her strongest tendencies were sabotages of mental health. To know what's healthy and then do something unhealthy is to make health a game. To conscientiously apply the tools is to work on mental health.

Acting in a group-minded way means that health is a business. Being civil to others makes health a business.

Committing the tools to memory is business-like because the tools don't help if they are only in a book someplace. Practicing the program religiously is a way of making health a business. On the other hand, to disregard what is beneficial is to make mental health a game.

PART 8. PERSPECTIVE

"Who is narrow of vision cannot be large of heart." Chinese proverb

"A frog in a well does not know the great sea." Japanese proverb

"TAKE A TOTAL VIEW NOT A PARTIAL VIEW"[76]

Jeff suffers a minor injustice and assumes an entire institution is corrupt. Laura makes a mistake and decides her efforts are worthless. George argues with his wife and decides his marriage is over.

For health, these individuals should be cautious in forming conclusions. When they first look at a situation, they only look from a single viewpoint; a partial view. Such people are prone to find insecurity or injustice and to react before finding the context of an event. They see a small detail and miss *the big picture*. It is better to look at each situation from several viewpoints because seeing from another point of view improves insight. Jeff, Laura and George perform at a higher level when they see the total view before reacting.

Using the total view means assessing situations both up close and from a distance. Events that seemed to be of critical importance may be only a triviality seen from afar. Situations that are temporary and insignificant in nature should be taken with a grain of salt.

"…neither the whole of truth nor the whole of good is revealed to any single observer, although each observer gains a partial superiority of insight from the peculiar position in which he stands."   William James, U.S. psychologist

"TEMPER IS THE INTELLECTUAL BLINDNESS TO THE OTHER SIDE OF THE STORY."[77]

How many sides are there to a story? At least two. A Japanese filmmaker created a film, *Rashomom,* where a story was told from many perspectives. Each spectator told a markedly different tale about what had happened.

A person may become angry when missing the other human's point of view. Empathy is the ability to see with another's eyes.

How many of us have cursed the driver ahead of us in a traffic jam?   That other driver has his own story to tell. He is in the same traffic jam we are in. He may be young and aggressive while we are not. Or we are young and aggressive and the other driver is not. There may be an accident ahead he sees and we can't yet see.

Maybe someone is ill and makes a mistake. Or the person is caring for a loved one and is distracted when we need assistance. Temper is sometimes deserved. But there are a great many times when the other person's story would moderate our feelings.

"I was taught that the way of progress is neither swift nor easy." Marie Curie, scientist

"COMPARE YOURSELF WITH YOURSELF"[78]

Many have the temptation to compare themselves with other people. This doesn't help because people vary greatly. Some have a high average performance, some a low average. In addition, it is impossible to precisely appraise everybody else.

The tool is to compare your performance with your own average. In each group example, the person giving an example compares his performance with how he would have done before learning the method. Hostile Julio, for example, can gage his progress when he compares himself with his own average.

PART 9. OTHER RECOVERY METHOD IDEAS

"STRONG LINKS AND WEAK LINKS"[79]

What does the program mean by strong links? The symptoms over which we have the least control are the strong links. They include responses that are hard to change. What are weak links? Other symptoms are easier to attack. The symptoms are milder. These are weak links.

We are able to use self-leadership on the weak links easily. We get relief from symptoms quickly. Effort applied to strong links is not as effective at first.

The strategy should be to apply self-leadership to weak links as much as possible in order to gain control of symptoms. By doing this, we develop emotional facility and improved confidence.

With patience, we can apply the tools to our strong links. The longer we try the better the results. It does take tenacity. Eventually the effort will produce results even in difficult areas.

"To feel brave, act as if you were brave…and a courage fit will very likely replace the fit of fear." William James, U.S. psychologist, philosopher

"WEAR THE MASK"[80]

TOM'S COMMENT: In the past, I would display my fears and anger. Anyone who saw me could tell which symptoms were affecting me. I made no effort to control expressions of fear or anger. I wore my emotions on my sleeve.

I learned from the program that I could do better by not giving outer expression to all my symptoms. By not displaying fear, I have felt less apprehension. When I don't make a show of being angry, my anger subsides sooner. The people I deal with are not as defensive.

***

Tom practiced acting with courage even when he felt afraid. As a result, he felt more confident.

The theory goes so far as to suggest that some exaggerate symptoms in order to impress others with the special, profound nature of their emotions. By avoiding theatrical presentation of symptoms, Tom is less apt to try to impress others.

William James, the first U.S. psychologist, was correct. When acting nervously, a person feels nervous. By displaying less trepidation, Tom feels a reduced amount of fear. The use of self-control in this instance boosts confidence.

"The more opinions you have, the less you see." Wim Wenders, German filmmaker. *Evening Standard* (London, 25 April 1990)

"Don't seek reality; just put an end to opinions." Zen proverb

"USE OBJECTIVITY"[81]

GLEN'S COMMENT: As a tense guy, I have an imagination that is too strong. I make too many subjective conclusions that upset me. My evaluation of people and events is personal and is affected by my imagination. Some of my opinions also reflect insecurity. I have learned that I can limit the excitation of my emotions with objectivity.

***

You can be objective when you use facts, data and measurements to define the environment. Examples of objectivity:

The dress is blue.
The floor has 138 tiles.
My checking account has $3.12 in it.
Water is composed of hydrogen and oxygen.
To be objective, you can describe the physical characteristics of objects. You can quantify items. You can repeat a mantra 200 times. A human being can read about

math, history and science. There are crossword puzzles. There are sudoku puzzles.

Subjectivity, on the other hand, can produce egocentricity, anger, vanity, fears and insecurity. Objectivity creates none of these emotions. Objectivity moves people away from unhealthy emotions that detract from health.

Glen doesn't have to worry about becoming too objective. He won't become a robot. In fact, he has trouble being objective enough.

Since you can only think one thought at a time it is often better to use objective thought to remain calm. Objective thinking allows people to see things calmly.

"Healing is a matter of time, but it is sometimes also a matter of opportunity." Hippocrates

"ACCEPT THE AUTHORITY OF THE PROFESSIONAL"[82]

Sometimes we do not trust our doctors or therapists. At times, we doubt what a professional is telling us. What should we do in such a situation? Where there is a conflict, we should respect the authority of the health professional.

Of course, we can provide symptoms to the doctor or therapist. We should let the professional know if the treatment seems to cause harm. We could get a second opinion, if necessary.

Furthermore, some of us self-diagnose. A physical symptom can inflame the imagination with insecurity. Rather than diagnosing ourselves, we should value the opinion of a health professional. The doctor or therapist trains to provide care to those in need and we should respect the knowledge and training of an expert.

"LIFE BY THE YARD IS HARD; LIFE BY THE INCH IS A CINCH"

Anxiety patients often look into the future and find situations to worry about. Such people can limit their insecurity by focusing on the present as much as possible. The longer you look into the future, the more potential pitfalls can be found.

We can limit insecurities if we focus on the near-term. If we consider the next couple of hours or the rest of the day, we can function without expanding our area of concern. The technique helps us in the short run. The tool contributes to relaxation over time.

"To know but not to act is not to know at all." Wang Yang-Ming (1472-1529)

"SABOTAGE"[83]

Low wrote many chapters about sabotage. The physician described different situations that he felt were sabotage. Simply, sabotage is to realize what is good thinking or good behavior and then to do something else.

The idea is that it is not enough to learn which thinking or behavior is helpful. The person has to be determined to think or behave correctly.

You avoid sabotage by making the effort to do what is healthy. That includes avoiding temperamental language. It includes utilizing diplomacy and group orientation. You avoid sabotage when choosing to follow the program.

"Those who have one foot in the canoe, and one foot in the boat, are going to fall into the river." Native American proverb

DUALITY AND SPONTANEITY[84]

What is duality in the Recovery Method? A human considers two different actions, often because of fear or anger. The mind is contemplating two different movements to the body. Without a clear intention the person is tentative. This is the idea of *duality*. Symptoms include self-consciousness and tenseness.

We work toward *spontaneity* when we hold only one secure thought in our mind. The secure thought is obtained by making a decision. By having one unambiguous intention we are less apprehensive. With less tenseness, we can act with less hesitation and more resolve.

Stigma: "…the most formidable obstacle to future progress in the arena of mental illness and health." U.S. Surgeon General's 1999 Report on Mental Health

STIGMA[85]

Stigma is the concept that a person with an emotional issue is inferior to others.   Some people, who are not educated, hold the idea that people with emotional concerns should be avoided. Dealing with stigma is important for those with nervous and anger problems. There is news in the media about patients who do wrong but patients who work and contribute aren't mentioned in the news. This isn't newsworthy.

Abraham Low made a few observations about stigma. One, is that stigma contributes to self-consciousness and self-doubt. The other, is that patients may fear recovery from illness because such recovery confirms the nature of a condition as psychological.

Mental health organizations in civilized countries are working to fight stigma by educating the public. Progress is slow. Stigma continues to be a problem patients have to confront.

Another idea is that a human doesn't choose to suffer a fear or anger condition. It is not something a person wants to have. Nobody should blame himself for a condition he didn't choose to have.

BRIEF BIOGRAPHY OF LOW

Abraham Low was born on February 28, 1891, in a corner of Poland that was part of the Austrian Empire. Low's father abused alcohol and had a violent temper. The boy's mother died when he was young. Low was high-strung as a youth but brilliant.

Because of family circumstances he and his siblings lived in an orphanage or with relatives. At school Low excelled in four languages besides his native German. He attended medical school at the University of Vienna where he learned Freudian psychoanalysis.

In 1921, Low moved to New York where he received his U.S. license to practice medicine. In 1923, he moved to the Chicago area where his sister lived. Low practiced psychoanalysis and joined the faculty of the University of Illinois Medical School. In 1935, he married Mae Willett and later had two daughters, Phyllis and Marilyn.

The doctor practiced Freudian psychoanalysis but had mediocre results with this method. His experience practicing in hospitals led him to reject psychoanalysis as a viable therapy for the seriously ill. The doctor developed his own ideas and put them into practice with impressive results.

Low's application of his own ideas led to bad feelings with some of the medical and academic establishment of that era. (Freudian therapies are used by a minority of therapists today.)

In 1937, Low founded Recovery Incorporated as a self-help organization. He made speeches, conducted group sessions, wrote articles and developed his method. His books include *Mental Health through Will Training, Peace versus Power in the Family, Selections from Dr. Low's Works* and *Manage Your Fears, Manage Your Anger* (a transcription of his speeches.)

Low died in 1954. Before his death, he turned the management of Recovery Incorporated over to his patients. The organization was later renamed Recovery International.

PART 10.   GROUP METHOD EXAMPLES

EXAMPLE FORMAT

Group examples usually cover routine events of everyday life. Emotional self-leadership developed on trivialities is applicable to bigger events. Sometimes, an everyday triviality can cause a lot of distress.

If a person wants help to find tools to use on a problem, the person can offer an *"I need help example."*

The example has the following elements:

1. The event that produced symptoms. (Not a long, complex story.)

2. The physical and mental symptoms the event produced.

3. The spotting of tools which apply to the problem. Did the person endorse?

4. What the person would have done before Recovery training.

Comments should spot the Recovery tools that apply to the symptoms. Members should only offer Recovery spotting (tools) not personal advice as to what another should do in a situation. The person giving the example should listen to the tools submitted, not remark extensively on his own example.

EXAMPLE 1

MARIA: I was out visiting someone who had a new litter of puppies. I picked up a puppy and the owner said, "Look out! You are hurting the puppy."

I was startled and dropped the puppy. I felt hot and my face turned red. I felt anger at the woman who spoke to me. I was also fearful that I might have hurt the puppy after I was startled.

I spotted that it was probable that the dog was OK. I chose to accept the dog's owner at her own average. I spoke to the dog's owner without aggression. I did not tell many people about the incident. I endorsed for the effort.

Before Recovery, I would have been more upset and told many people about the incident.

KAREN: Maria chose "peace over power."
DAVE: Maria replaced an insecure thought with a secure thought.
DEBBIE: I spot control of perfectionism. Maria accepted the dog owner at her own average.
BOB: Maria controlled her processing. She didn't talk about the event to excite herself.
ANN: Maria had the will to bear discomfort. Comfort is a want, not a need.
KAREN: The symptoms were distressing but not dangerous.
JAMAL: I spot she excused herself rather than accused herself.
KAREN: Maria was self-led, not symptom-led.
MARIA: Thanks for the comments.

EXAMPLE 2

JIM: I was teaching a college class at a local college. A student attended the first session. I did not see her during the lectures that followed. She did show up to take the final exam after missing all the classes in between.

When I saw her, I had angry temper directed at her. At first, I felt she was acting this way to insult me. I also had a fear that I wasn't authorized to do anything about the situation.

I spotted that I could accept her at her own average. I embraced the secure thought that I could set my own class rules. I spoke to her civilly in private and told her she couldn't take the test. I endorsed for the effort.

Before I knew Recovery, I might have been angrier. I would have been afraid of asserting myself for fear of causing a scene. I would have let her take the test even though it was inappropriate.

MARILYN: Jim asserted himself without aggression.
TOM: He accepted the student at her own average.
PAT: People do things that irritate us, not to irritate us.
JOANN: Jim had the will to bear discomfort.
CURTIS: The outer environment can be rude, crude and indifferent.
VIRGINIA: Jim replaced his insecure thoughts with secure thoughts.
MARILYN: Jim chose peace over power.

EXAMPLE 3

BILL: I purchased an expensive lawn tractor. When it arrived, I noticed that the tractor required some adjustments before I could use it. I was disappointed. I felt some anger that the tractor was delivered in this condition. I was capable of making the adjustments myself but decided to contact the dealer. I was civil with the dealer who agreed to adjust the tractor. If this didn't work, I was going to contact the manufacturer. I endorsed for the effort.

Before Recovery, I would have been angrier. I might have worked on the tractor myself to avoid asserting myself. If I had talked to the dealer, I might have been aggressive.

LINDA: Bill asserted himself with culture.
ROBERT: Bill was self-led instead of symptom led.
FRITZ: Bill chose peace over power with the dealer.
LINDA: I spot the will to bear discomfort.
ROBBIE: Bill acted with culture.
JUANITA: Bill controlled his perfectionism and accepted the company at its own average.
ROBERT: People do things that irritate us, not to irritate us.
ROBBIE: Bill used part acts to work on the situation.
BILL: Thanks for the comments.

RECOVERY INTERNATIONAL

1415 W. 22nd St.
Tower Floor
Oak Brook, IL 60523
(866) 221-0302
Or (312) 337-5661

http://www.recoveryinternational.org is the current website. The website contains a listing of the group meetings by region. There is also a group on Facebook.

Nervous patients run the organization and the local support groups. The organization is self-supporting and accepts donations.

About the Author

Robert Courtade served in the U.S. Army during the Viet Nam era. After the service he became a computer operator and later an award winning computer specialist for the Department of Defense. He retired in 1996.
Robert was referred to Recovery International is 1985. He has been active in the self-help program and its meetings ever since.
The author's email address is   rcourtade@hotmail.com .

Book Discounts

Paperback Deep Discounts **abridged** version available at website:

https://www.createspace.com/6185111

Discount Code is: ZA8ZU8DK

Paperback Deep Discounts **long** version available at website:

https://www.createspace.com/3344975

Discount Code is: R6F24XFN

Due to cookies, each book must be ordered from a different computer.

Endorse for reading the book!

If you like the book, please review on Amazon.com

INDEX

Notes

1   The system created by combining the techniques used at Recovery International meetings. The techniques were developed by Abraham A. Low, M.D.

2   *Manage Your Fears, Manage You're Anger: A Psychiatrist Speaks* (A transcription of lectures by Dr. Abraham A. Low), c.1995, Willett Publishing Co., Glencoe, Il 60022, p.185-186

3   *Mental Health through Will Training*, c. 1997, Willett Publishing Company, Glencoe, Il 60022, p.46-50

4   MHTWT, p. 26, 43-60; MYF, MYA, p.37, 42

5   MHTWT, p. 26-27, 33-42; MYF, MYA, p.37,42

6   MYF, MYA, p.135-141, 261-269

7   MHTWT, p.26-27, 56-60

8   MYF, MYA, p. 161, 163, 203, 202-207; MHTWT, p.29,133, 150, 155, 163-167, 169, 189-190, 203-204, 227,233-234,257-258, 305-310, *Selections from Dr. Low's Works*, Recovery Inc., Chicago, Il, p. 40-43, 80-84

9   MHTWT, p. 306-308, term is used in the oral tradition of Recovery Inc.

10   Recited at Recovery meetings.   MHTWT, p. 219-220

11   MHTWT, p.65, 68, 146,329,330,334; usually orally cited as: "Commanded the muscles to do the thing he feared to do." at many Recovery meetings.

12   MHTWT p. 25

13   The term Temperamental lingo is usually used at Recovery meetings. Dr. Low referred to it as "Temperamental Lingo." MHTWT, p. 26-27,42,169,295,363,431-433

14   Cited at Recovery meetings. Term is also used outside Recovery ; MYF, MYA, p. 323 refers to "low mood." MHTWT p. 96 'low feelings'. "Lowered feelings" a term of A. A. Low, M.D.

15   Recited at Recovery meetings. Concept discussed in MHTWT p.182-184

16   MHTWT p.159-161, 169-173, 240-242, 321-322. MYA p. 363-364. Recited at Recovery meetings.

17   Slogan recited at Recovery meetings. Concept in MYF, MYA p.245-246, *PEACE versus POWER in the FAMILY*, c. 1967, Willett Publishing Co. p.195, Selections p.31

18   MHTWT p. 108-110, 362 MYF, MYA p.93-100 Also recited at Recovery meetings

19   MHTWT p.253-258, 256-257, 390. Peace vs. Power p.137, 148. MYF, MYA p.224. Selections p.81

20   This is recited at Recovery meetings, concept is in MHTWT p.74-79, 151 Peace vs. Power p.103

21   MHTWT p.162-167, MYF, MYA p.30-34, 196-200.
22   Selections p. 46
23   Selections, p. 45-47. . Endorse, endorsement and endorsing are cited at Recovery meetings.
24   Saying is orally cited at Recovery meetings. Concept was explored in MHTWT, p. 191-196 Also MYF, MYA p.249-256, 270-275, Selections p. 81
25   Occasionally mentioned at meetings. Peace vs. Power p.47-51, 79, 108-109. MHTWT p.256-257
26   Recited at Recovery Inc. meetings MHTWT p.61-70, 325-334 MYF, MYA p.114-118, 312-315, 330-338
27   MHTWT p. 64-70. Recited at Recovery meetings.
28   MHTWT p. 67
29   MYF, MYA p.312-315, 324-325. Heard only occasionally at Recovery meetings.
30   MHTWT p. 374
31   The term is mentioned at Recovery meetings. MHTWT p368-375
32   MHTWT, p. 80-86, 211, 246-252, 416   MYF, MYA, p.18-21, 73-76,119-127,170-176
33   MHTWT, p. 80, 83-86, 103, 110, 211-212, 248-252, 416 also MYF, MYA p.73-76, 170-176
34   PEACE versus POWER, p. 41
35   Saying is orally recited at Recovery meetings. Also "Replace an insecure thought with a secure thought." MYF, MYA Lecture 1: "There Are Two Choices: Security and Insecurity. MHTWT, p.42, 135,380-381
36   Recited at Recovery meetings. Also "Sensations are distressing but not dangerous." MHTWT p.115-116, 118, 119. Selections p. 112
37   MHTWT p.140, 430 Recited at Recovery meetings.
38   Selections, p.92-94. Occasionally cited at Recovery meetings.
39   Slogan is recited at Recovery meetings. Decisions discussed MHTWT p.33-34, 36-42, 242, 247-250
40   Recited at Recovery meetings. MHTWT p. 34, 246-252. MYF,MYA p.60, 220-225
41   The saying is recited at Recovery meetings. MYF, MYA p.147-156. MHTWT p. 87-88, 153
42   The saying is recited at Recovery meetings. MHTWT p.115-119, MYF, MYA p.77-80.
43   Concept discussed MHTWT p.91-100, 368-375 MYF, MYA p.184, 342-357
44   MHTWT p.95-100
45   MHTWT p. 278
46   The saying is recited at meetings. Concept MHTWT p.181, 212; MYF,MYA p. 241, 426, 430
47   Cited at Recovery meetings. Averageness: MHTWT, p. 80, 83-86, 103, 110, 211-212, 248-252, 416; MYF, MYA p.73-76, 170-176

[48]   MYF, MYA p.81-87, 177-183, 212-213 Recited at meetings.

[49]   Selections, p. 35, MYF, MYA p. 298-304

[50]   Saying recited at Recovery meetings. Apparently from Abraham A. Low

[51]   The oral saying is recited at Recovery meetings. The concept is discussed in PEACE vs. POWER., p. 195 Also MYF, MYA p.110

[52]   Recited at Recovery meetings. MHTWT p. 106-108, 231. MYA p. 253-255. Hurt to self-importance: Selections p.50 .

[53]   MHTWT p.57-60. "Choose fellowship over sovereignty" occasionally recited.

[54]   Recited at Recovery meetings, concept explored MHTWT p.107-109, 221-223, 392-397 MYF, MYA p.298-302.

[55]   Saying is recited at Recovery meetings. The saying encapsulates the ideas of Abraham A. Low

[56]   Saying is used at Recovery meetings. St. Augustine used the phrase. MHTWT p. 21; MYA p. 228

[57]   Saying is recited at Recovery meetings. MHTWT p. 253

[58]   The Recovery slogans are recited at the meetings. MYA p. 189-195, 355-356. MHTWT p.253 discusses asserting without temper. Concept in Peace vs. Power p.45

[59]   MHTWT p.261-269   Occasionally cited at Recovery meetings.

[60]   Temper expression discussed in MHTWT, p. 76-78, 177,178

[61]   Discomfort saying usually cited as "He/She had the will to bear discomfort" at meetings. MHTWT p. 145-149, 219

[62]   The saying is recited at Recovery meetings. MHTWT p.147-148, 219, 220. MYF, MYA p. 273, 284-289.

[63]   The saying is recited at Recovery meetings. Concept is discussed MYF, MYA p.237-243.

[64]   The saying is recited at Recovery meetings. Abraham A. Low wrote extensively about comfort and discomfort.

[65]   The saying is recited at Recovery meetings. Concept: MHTWT p. 149.

[66]   Saying is recited at Recovery meetings. MHTWT p.146-147 refers to "face, tolerate and endure."

[67]   Saying recited at Recovery meetings. Concept discussed MHTWT p.135-138, 380.

[68]   The self-leadership saying is recited at Recovery meetings. Concept is explored in MHTWT p.228-239, 281-282, 291 MYF, MYA p.114-118, 280-283, 237-243. Peace vs. Power p.186.

[69]   Recited at Recovery meetings. MHTWT p.106-110 MYF, MYA p.53-56

[70]   MHTWT p.106, Selections p.31-32

[71]   The saying is recited at Recovery meetings. MHTWT p.162-167.

MYA p. 198.

[72]   The saying is recited at Recovery meetings. Concept: MHTWT p.201

[73]   Saying is recited at Recovery meetings. Concept discussed MHTWT p.237, 243, 246-249, 288-289; Selections p.45-46

[74]   Saying is recited at Recovery meetings. MHTWT p.42, 415. MYF, MYA p.339-341.

[75]   The saying is recited at Recovery meetings. MHTWT p.214-220

[76]   The saying is recited at Recovery meetings. MHTWT p.208-214 MYF, MYA p.101-106.

[77]   The saying is recited at Recovery meetings. MHTWT p.159

[78]   The saying is recited at some Recovery meetings. Phrased used my martial arts instructors and others outside Recovery

[79]   Tool is recited at Recovery meetings. Concept discussed MHTWT p.62, 366, 376-384

[80]   The saying has been recited at Recovery meetings. Former saying was "Wear the mask." The concept is explored in MHTWT p.187-190, 322.

[81]   Saying recited at Recovery meetings. Also "Be objective not subjective." MHTWT p.126-130, 289

[82]   Saying is recited at Recovery meetings. MHTWT p.279-294

[83]   MHTWT p.279-294, 305-310, 325-334

[84]   Mentioned at Recovery meetings. MHTWT p. 95, 243, 249, 410-416. MYF, MYA p.116-117, 165-167, 193; Selections p. 94-96

[85]   MHTWT p. 22, 207, 272-273, 276-277, 293, 297, 408-409

Made in the USA
Middletown, DE
29 December 2017